Belongs To

2020

Has been a surprising year. Looking back with a grateful heart in acceptance of all the twists and turns I choose to reflect on my successes and failures in gratitude.

In the lined space write down what you experienced and your takeaways.

Be true to yourself and grow!

Soar to new heights in 2021

Write your intentions for the coming year and make sure you write them as though they have already come to pass. Dive into the emotional space of the wish fulfilled, see it, taste it, smell it, touch it and it is so....

2021

Year At A Glance

JANUARY

MON	TUE	WED	THU	FRI	SAT	SUN
				01	02	03
04	05	06	07	08	09	10
11	12	13	14	15	16	17
18	19	20	21	22	23	24
25	26	27	28	29	30	31

FEBRUARY

MON	TUE	WED	THU	FRI	SAT	SUN
01	02	03	04	05	06	07
08	09	10	11	12	13	14
15	16	17	18	19	20	21
22	23	24	25	26	27	28

MARCH

MON	TUE	WED	THU	FRI	SAT	SU
01	02	03	04	05	06	07
08	09	10	11	12	13	14
15	16	17	18	19	20	21
22	23	24	25	26	27	28
29	30	31				

APRIL

MON	TUE	WED	THU	FRI	SAT	SUN
			01	02	03	04
05	06	07	08	09	10	11
12	13	14	15	16	17	18
19	20	21	22	23	24	25
26	27	28	29	30		

MAY

MON	TUE	WED	THU	FRI	SAT	SUN
					01	02
03	04	05	06	07	08	09
10	11	12	13	14	15	16
17	18	19	20	21	22	23
24	25	26	27	28	29	30
31						

JUNE

MON	TUE	WED	THU	FRI	SAT	SU
	01	02	03	04	05	06
07	08	09	10	11	12	13
14	15	16	17	18	19	20
21	22	23	24	25	26	27
28	29	30				

JULY

MON	TUE	WED	THU	FRI	SAT	SUN
			01	02	03	04
05	06	07	08	09	10	11
12	13	14	15	16	17	18
19	20	21	22	23	24	25
26	27	28	29	30	31	

AUGUST

MON	TUE	WED	THU	FRI	SAT	SUN
						01
02	03	04	05	06	07	08
09	10	11	12	13	14	15
16	17	18	19	20	21	22
23	24	25	26	27	28	29
30	31					

SEPTEMBER

MON	TUE	WED	THU	FRI	SAT	SU
		01	02	03	04	05
06	07	08	09	10	11	12
13	14	15	16	17	18	19
20	21	22	23	24	25	26
27	28	29	30			

OCTOBER

MON	TUE	WED	THU	FRI	SAT	SUN
				01	02	03
04	05	06	07	08	09	10
11	12	13	14	15	16	17
18	19	20	21	22	23	24
25	26	27	28	29	30	31

NOVEMBER

MON	TUE	WED	THU	FRI	SAT	SUN
01	02	03	04	05	06	07
08	09	10	11	12	13	14
15	16	17	18	19	20	21
22	23	24	25	26	27	28
29	30					

DECEMBER

MON	TUE	WED	THU	FRI	SAT	SU
		01	02	03	04	05
06	07	08	09	10	11	12
13	14	15	16	17	18	19
20	21	22	23	24	25	26
27	28	29	30	31		

Lunar Calendar 2021

UNIVERSAL TIME COORDINATED

Last Quarter	*New Moon*	*First Quarter*	*Full Moon*
JAN 6 - 9:38 AM	JAN 13 - 5:02 AM	JAN 20 - 9:03 PM	JAN 28 - 7:18 PM
FEB 4 - 5:38 PM	FEB 11 - 7:08 PM	FEB 19 - 6:49 PM	FEB 27 - 8:19 AM
MAR 6 - 1:32 AM	MAR 13 10:23 AM	MAR 21 - 2:41 PM	MAR 28 - 6:50 PM
APR 4 - 10:04 AM	APR 12 - 2:32 AM	APR 20 - 7:00 AM	APR 27 - 3:33 AM
MAY 3 - 7:51 PM	MAY 11 - 7:01 PM	MAY 19 - 7:13 PM	MAY 26 - 11:14 AM
JUN 2 - 7:26 AM	JUN 10 - 10:54 AM	JUN 18 - 3:54 AM	JUN 24 - 6:40 PM
JUL 1 - 9:12 PM / JUL 31 - 1:18 PM	JUL 10 1:17 AM	JUL 17 10:11 AM	JUL 24 - 2:37 AM
AUG 8 - 1:50 PM	AUG 15 - 3:21 PM	AUG 22 - 12:02 PM	AUG 30 - 7:15 AM
SEP 7 - 12:52 AM	SEP 13 - 8:41 PM	SEP 20 - 11:54 PM	SEO 29 - 1:58 AM
OCT 6 - 11:05 AM	OCT 13 - 3:27 AM	OCT 20 - 2:57 PM	OCT 28 - 8:06 PM
NOV 4 - 9:15 PM	NOV 11 - 12:48 PM	NOV 19 - 8:59 AM	NOV 27 - 12:29 PM
DEC 4 - 7:44 AM	DEC 11 - 1:37 AM	DEC 19 - 4:37 AM	DEC 27 - 2:26 AM

U.S. Federal Holidays

Important Dates

NEW YEAR'S DAY	Friday, January 1st
MARTIN LUTHER KING JR. DAY	Monday, January 18th
PRESIDENT'S DAY	Monday, February 15th
MEMORIAL DAY	Monday, May 31st
INDEPENDENCE DAY	Monday, July 5th
LABOR DAY	Monday, September 6th
COLUMBUS DAY	Monday, October 11th
VETERAN'S DAY	Thursday, November 11th
THANKSGIVING DAY	Thursday, November 25th
CHRISTMAS DAY	Friday, December 24th
NEW YEAR'S DAY	Friday, December 31st

UNIVERSAL TIME COORDINATED

Wheel Of The Year

IMBOLIC (EARLY SPRING)	Moday, February 1st
OSTARA (SPRING EQUINOX)	Saturday, March 20 - 9:37 AM
BELTANE (HIGH SPRING)	Saturday, May 1st
LITHA (SUMMER SOLSTICE)	Monday, June 21 - 3:32 AM
LAMMAS/LUGHNASADH (SUMMER SOLSTICE)	Sunday, August 1st
MABON (DEEP AUTUMN)	Wednesday, September 22 7:21 PM
SAMHAIN (DEEP AUTUMN)	Sunday, October 31st
YULE (WINTER SOLSTICE)	Tuesday, December 21 3:59 PM

WEBSITES	USER	PASSWORDS

TAKE
THE DAY
AND LEAVE US
THE MOON
AND WE WILL SEIZE
THE NIGHT
ATTICUS

January 2021

DECEMBER 2020

MON	TUE	WED	THU	FRI	SAT	SUN
	01	02	03	04	05	06
07	08	09	10	11	12	13
14	15	16	17	18	19	20
21	22	23	24	25	26	27
28	29	30	31			

MONDAY	TUESDAY	WEDNESDAY	THURSDAY	FRIDAY	SATURDAY	SUNDAY
				01	02	03
04	05	06	07	08	09	10
11	12	13	14	15	16	17
18	19	20	21	22	23	24
25	26	27	28	29	30	31

FEBRUARY

MON	TUE	WED	THU	FRI	SAT	SUN
01	02	03	04	05	06	07
08	09	10	11	12	13	14
15	16	17	18	19	20	21
22	23	24	25	26	27	28

BIRTHSTONE: Garnet

ZOIDIAC SIGN: Dec. 22- Jan 19th Capricorn
Jan 20th - Feb 18th Aquarius

BIRTH MONTH FLOWER: Carnation & Snowdrop

Spiritual Goals

Intentions

Astrological Events

Card of the Mo.

I am grateful for

I am

To Do

- [ ]
- [ ]
- [ ]
- [ ]
- [ ]
- [ ]
- [ ]

To Buy

- [ ]
- [ ]
- [ ]
- [ ]
- [ ]
- [ ]
- [ ]

12/28 MONDAY

12/29 TUESDAY

12/30 WEDNESDAY

12/31 THURSDAY

WEEKLY PLANNER

01/01 FRIDAY

☐ ______
☐ ______
☐ ______
☐ ______
☐ ______
☐ ______
☐ ______
☐ ______
☐ ______
☐ ______
☐ ______
☐ ______
☐ ______
☐ ______
☐ ______

01/02 SATURDAY

☐ ______
☐ ______
☐ ______
☐ ______
☐ ______
☐ ______

01/03 SUNDAY

☐ ______
☐ ______
☐ ______
☐ ______
☐ ______
☐ ______

APPOINTMENTS

NOTES

TRACKER

	S	M	T	W	T	F	S
______	☐	☐	☐	☐	☐	☐	☐
______	☐	☐	☐	☐	☐	☐	☐
______	☐	☐	☐	☐	☐	☐	☐
______	☐	☐	☐	☐	☐	☐	☐
______	☐	☐	☐	☐	☐	☐	☐
______	☐	☐	☐	☐	☐	☐	☐

01/04 MONDAY

- [ ]
- [ ]
- [ ]
- [ ]
- [ ]
- [ ]
- [ ]
- [ ]
- [ ]
- [ ]
- [ ]
- [ ]
- [ ]
- [ ]
- [ ]

01/05 TUESDAY

- [ ]
- [ ]
- [ ]
- [ ]
- [ ]
- [ ]
- [ ]
- [ ]
- [ ]
- [ ]
- [ ]
- [ ]
- [ ]
- [ ]
- [ ]

01/06 WEDNESDAY

- [ ]
- [ ]
- [ ]
- [ ]
- [ ]
- [ ]
- [ ]
- [ ]
- [ ]
- [ ]
- [ ]
- [ ]
- [ ]
- [ ]
- [ ]
- [ ]

01/07 THURSDAY

- [ ]
- [ ]
- [ ]
- [ ]
- [ ]
- [ ]
- [ ]
- [ ]
- [ ]
- [ ]
- [ ]
- [ ]
- [ ]
- [ ]
- [ ]
- [ ]

WEEKLY PLANNER

01/08 FRIDAY

- [ ]
- [ ]
- [ ]
- [ ]
- [ ]
- [ ]
- [ ]
- [ ]
- [ ]
- [ ]
- [ ]
- [ ]
- [ ]
- [ ]
- [ ]

01/09 SATURDAY

- [ ]
- [ ]
- [ ]
- [ ]
- [ ]
- [ ]

01/10 SUNDAY

- [ ]
- [ ]
- [ ]
- [ ]
- [ ]
- [ ]

APPOINTMENTS

NOTES

TRACKER

	S	M	T	W	T	F	S
	☐	☐	☐	☐	☐	☐	☐
	☐	☐	☐	☐	☐	☐	☐
	☐	☐	☐	☐	☐	☐	☐
	☐	☐	☐	☐	☐	☐	☐
	☐	☐	☐	☐	☐	☐	☐
	☐	☐	☐	☐	☐	☐	☐

01/11 MONDAY

01/12 TUESDAY

01/13 WEDNESDAY

01/14 THURSDAY

WEEKLY PLANNER

01/15 FRIDAY

01/16 SATURDAY

01/17 SUNDAY

APPOINTMENTS

NOTES

TRACKER

	S	M	T	W	T	F	S

01/18 MONDAY

- [ ]
- [ ]
- [ ]
- [ ]
- [ ]
- [ ]
- [ ]
- [ ]
- [ ]
- [ ]
- [ ]
- [ ]
- [ ]
- [ ]
- [ ]

01/19 TUESDAY

- [ ]
- [ ]
- [ ]
- [ ]
- [ ]
- [ ]
- [ ]
- [ ]
- [ ]
- [ ]
- [ ]
- [ ]
- [ ]
- [ ]
- [ ]

01/20 WEDNESDAY

- [ ]
- [ ]
- [ ]
- [ ]
- [ ]
- [ ]
- [ ]
- [ ]
- [ ]
- [ ]
- [ ]
- [ ]
- [ ]
- [ ]
- [ ]
- [ ]

01/21 THURSDAY

- [ ]
- [ ]
- [ ]
- [ ]
- [ ]
- [ ]
- [ ]
- [ ]
- [ ]
- [ ]
- [ ]
- [ ]
- [ ]
- [ ]
- [ ]
- [ ]

WEEKLY PLANNER

01/22 FRIDAY

- [ ]
- [ ]
- [ ]
- [ ]
- [ ]
- [ ]
- [ ]
- [ ]
- [ ]
- [ ]
- [ ]
- [ ]
- [ ]
- [ ]
- [ ]

01/23 SATURDAY

- [ ]
- [ ]
- [ ]
- [ ]
- [ ]
- [ ]

01/24 SUNDAY

- [ ]
- [ ]
- [ ]
- [ ]
- [ ]
- [ ]

APPOINTMENTS

NOTES

TRACKER

	S	M	T	W	T	F	S
	☐	☐	☐	☐	☐	☐	☐
	☐	☐	☐	☐	☐	☐	☐
	☐	☐	☐	☐	☐	☐	☐
	☐	☐	☐	☐	☐	☐	☐
	☐	☐	☐	☐	☐	☐	☐
	☐	☐	☐	☐	☐	☐	☐

01/25 MONDAY

- [ ]
- [ ]
- [ ]
- [ ]
- [ ]
- [ ]
- [ ]
- [ ]
- [ ]
- [ ]
- [ ]
- [ ]
- [ ]
- [ ]
- [ ]

01/26 TUESDAY

- [ ]
- [ ]
- [ ]
- [ ]
- [ ]
- [ ]
- [ ]
- [ ]
- [ ]
- [ ]
- [ ]
- [ ]
- [ ]
- [ ]
- [ ]

01/27 WEDNESDAY

- [ ]
- [ ]
- [ ]
- [ ]
- [ ]
- [ ]
- [ ]
- [ ]
- [ ]
- [ ]
- [ ]
- [ ]
- [ ]
- [ ]
- [ ]
- [ ]

01/28 THURSDAY

- [ ]
- [ ]
- [ ]
- [ ]
- [ ]
- [ ]
- [ ]
- [ ]
- [ ]
- [ ]
- [ ]
- [ ]
- [ ]
- [ ]
- [ ]
- [ ]

WEEKLY PLANNER

01/29 FRIDAY

- [ ]
- [ ]
- [ ]
- [ ]
- [ ]
- [ ]
- [ ]
- [ ]
- [ ]
- [ ]
- [ ]
- [ ]
- [ ]
- [ ]
- [ ]

01/30 SATURDAY

- [ ]
- [ ]
- [ ]
- [ ]
- [ ]
- [ ]

01/31 SUNDAY

- [ ]
- [ ]
- [ ]
- [ ]
- [ ]
- [ ]

APPOINTMENTS

NOTES

TRACKER

	S	M	T	W	T	F	S
	☐	☐	☐	☐	☐	☐	☐
	☐	☐	☐	☐	☐	☐	☐
	☐	☐	☐	☐	☐	☐	☐
	☐	☐	☐	☐	☐	☐	☐
	☐	☐	☐	☐	☐	☐	☐
	☐	☐	☐	☐	☐	☐	☐

ALL THAT WE SEE OR SEEM IS BUT A DREAM WITHIN A DREAM

EDGAR ALLAN POE

February 2021

JANUARY

MON	TUE	WED	THU	FRI	SAT	SU
				01	02	03
04	05	06	07	08	09	10
11	12	13	14	15	16	17
18	19	20	21	22	23	24
25	26	27	28	29	30	31

MONDAY	TUESDAY	WEDNESDAY	THURSDAY	FRIDAY	SATURDAY	SUNDAY
01	02	03	04	05	06	0
08	09	10	11	12	13	1
15	16	17	18	19	20	2
22	23	24	25	26	27	2

MARCH

MON	TUE	WED	THU	FRI	SAT	SUN
01	02	03	04	05	06	07
08	09	10	11	12	13	14
15	16	17	18	19	20	21
22	23	24	25	26	27	28
29	30	31				

BIRTHSTONE: Amethyst

ZOIDIAC SIGN: Jan 20 - Feb 18th Aquarius
Feb 19 - Mar 20 Pisces

BIRTH MONTH FLOWER: Violet - Primrose

Spiritual Goals

Intentions

Astrological Events

Card of the Mo.

I am grateful for

___

___

___

I am

___

___

___

To Do

- [ ] ___
- [ ] ___
- [ ] ___
- [ ] ___
- [ ] ___
- [ ] ___
- [ ] ___

To Buy

- [ ] ___
- [ ] ___
- [ ] ___
- [ ] ___
- [ ] ___
- [ ] ___
- [ ] ___

02/01 MONDAY

02/02 TUESDAY

02/03 WEDNESDAY

02/04 THURSDAY

WEEKLY PLANNER

02/05 FRIDAY

02/06 SATURDAY

02/07 SUNDAY

APPOINTMENTS

NOTES

TRACKER

	S	M	T	W	T	F	S
	☐	☐	☐	☐	☐	☐	☐
	☐	☐	☐	☐	☐	☐	☐
	☐	☐	☐	☐	☐	☐	☐
	☐	☐	☐	☐	☐	☐	☐
	☐	☐	☐	☐	☐	☐	☐
	☐	☐	☐	☐	☐	☐	☐

02/08 MONDAY

02/09 TUESDAY

02/10 WEDNESDAY

02/11 THURSDAY

WEEKLY PLANNER

02/12 FRIDAY

- [ ]
- [ ]
- [ ]
- [ ]
- [ ]
- [ ]
- [ ]
- [ ]
- [ ]
- [ ]
- [ ]
- [ ]
- [ ]
- [ ]
- [ ]

02/13 SATURDAY

- [ ]
- [ ]
- [ ]
- [ ]
- [ ]
- [ ]

02/14 SUNDAY

- [ ]
- [ ]
- [ ]
- [ ]
- [ ]
- [ ]

APPOINTMENTS

NOTES

TRACKER

	S	M	T	W	T	F	S
	☐	☐	☐	☐	☐	☐	☐
	☐	☐	☐	☐	☐	☐	☐
	☐	☐	☐	☐	☐	☐	☐
	☐	☐	☐	☐	☐	☐	☐
	☐	☐	☐	☐	☐	☐	☐
	☐	☐	☐	☐	☐	☐	☐

02/15 MONDAY

02/16 TUESDAY

02/17 WEDNESDAY

02/18 THURSDAY

WEEKLY PLANNER

02/19 FRIDAY

- [ ]
- [ ]
- [ ]
- [ ]
- [ ]
- [ ]
- [ ]
- [ ]
- [ ]
- [ ]
- [ ]
- [ ]
- [ ]
- [ ]
- [ ]

02/20 SATURDAY

- [ ]
- [ ]
- [ ]
- [ ]
- [ ]
- [ ]

02/21 SUNDAY

- [ ]
- [ ]
- [ ]
- [ ]
- [ ]
- [ ]

APPOINTMENTS

NOTES

TRACKER

	S	M	T	W	T	F	S
	☐	☐	☐	☐	☐	☐	☐
	☐	☐	☐	☐	☐	☐	☐
	☐	☐	☐	☐	☐	☐	☐
	☐	☐	☐	☐	☐	☐	☐
	☐	☐	☐	☐	☐	☐	☐
	☐	☐	☐	☐	☐	☐	☐

02/22 MONDAY

02/23 TUESDAY

02/24 WEDNESDAY

02/25 THURSDAY

WEEKLY PLANNER

02/26 FRIDAY

02/27 SATURDAY

02/28 SUNDAY

APPOINTMENTS

NOTES

TRACKER

	S	M	T	W	T	F	S

THE TRUTH IS MAGIC
LIVES IN ALL OF US
WHO CHOOSE
TO LOOK FOR IT

ATTICUS

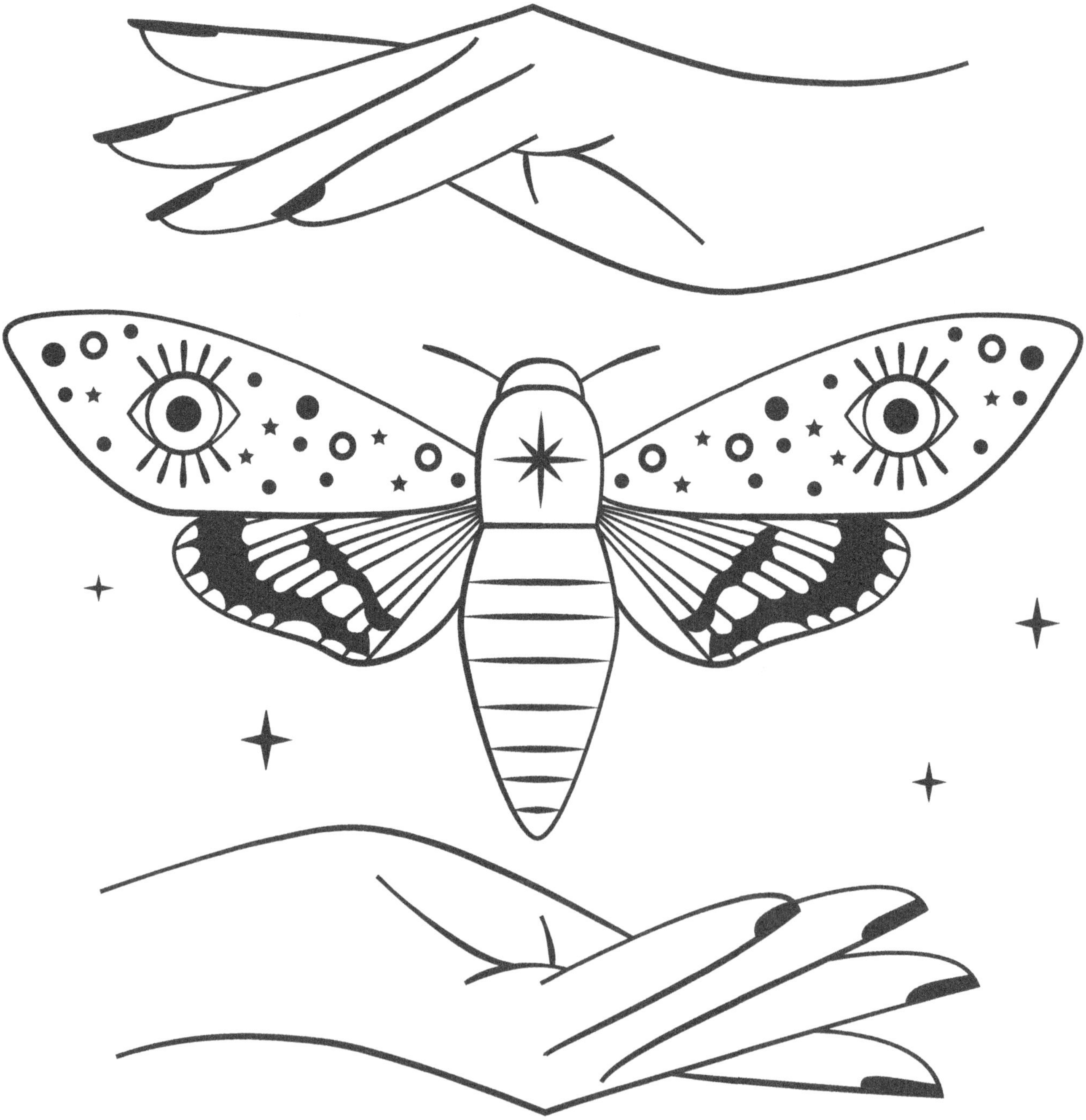

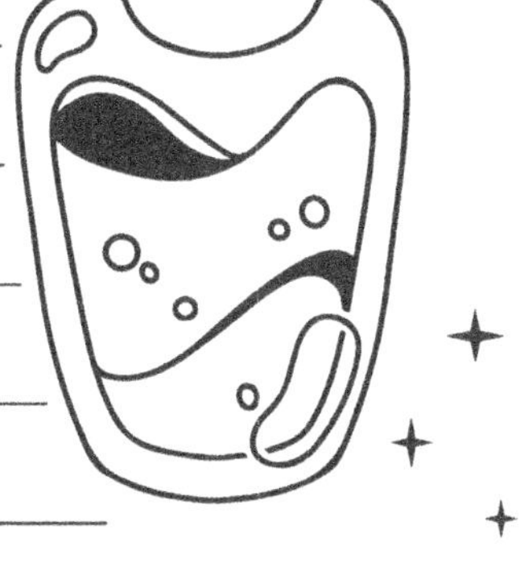

FEBRUARY

MON	TUE	WED	THU	FRI	SAT	SU
01	02	03	04	05	06	07
08	09	10	11	12	13	14
15	16	17	18	19	20	21
22	23	24	25	26	27	28

March 2021

MONDAY	TUESDAY	WEDNESDAY	THURSDAY	FRIDAY	SATURDAY	SUNDAY
01	02	03	04	05	06	0
08	09	10	11	12	13	1
15	16	17	18	19	20	2
22	23	24	25	26	27	2
29	30	31				

APRIL

MON	TUE	WED	THU	FRI	SAT	SUN
			01	02	03	04
05	06	07	08	09	10	11
12	13	14	15	16	17	18
19	20	21	22	23	24	25
26	27	28	29	30		

BIRTHSTONE: Aquamarine, Bloodstone

ZOIDIAC SIGN: Feb 19 - Mar 20 Pisces
Mar 21 - Apr 19 Aries

BIRTH MONTH FLOWER: Daffodil & Jonquil

Spiritual Goals

Intentions

Astrological Events

Card of the Mo.

I am grateful for

I am

To Do

- [ ]
- [ ]
- [ ]
- [ ]
- [ ]
- [ ]
- [ ]

To Buy

- [ ]
- [ ]
- [ ]
- [ ]
- [ ]
- [ ]
- [ ]

03/01 MONDAY

03/02 TUESDAY

03/03 WEDNESDAY

03/04 THURSDAY

WEEKLY PLANNER

03/05 FRIDAY

- [ ]
- [ ]
- [ ]
- [ ]
- [ ]
- [ ]
- [ ]
- [ ]
- [ ]
- [ ]
- [ ]
- [ ]
- [ ]
- [ ]
- [ ]

03/06 SATURDAY

- [ ]
- [ ]
- [ ]
- [ ]
- [ ]
- [ ]

03/07 SUNDAY

- [ ]
- [ ]
- [ ]
- [ ]
- [ ]
- [ ]

APPOINTMENTS

NOTES

TRACKER

	S	M	T	W	T	F	S
	☐	☐	☐	☐	☐	☐	☐
	☐	☐	☐	☐	☐	☐	☐
	☐	☐	☐	☐	☐	☐	☐
	☐	☐	☐	☐	☐	☐	☐
	☐	☐	☐	☐	☐	☐	☐
	☐	☐	☐	☐	☐	☐	☐

03/08 MONDAY

03/09 TUESDAY

03/10 WEDNESDAY

03/11 THURSDAY

WEEKLY PLANNER

03/12 FRIDAY

- [ ]
- [ ]
- [ ]
- [ ]
- [ ]
- [ ]
- [ ]
- [ ]
- [ ]
- [ ]
- [ ]
- [ ]
- [ ]
- [ ]
- [ ]

03/13 SATURDAY

- [ ]
- [ ]
- [ ]
- [ ]
- [ ]
- [ ]

03/14 SUNDAY

- [ ]
- [ ]
- [ ]
- [ ]
- [ ]
- [ ]

APPOINTMENTS

NOTES

TRACKER

	S	M	T	W	T	F	S
	☐	☐	☐	☐	☐	☐	☐
	☐	☐	☐	☐	☐	☐	☐
	☐	☐	☐	☐	☐	☐	☐
	☐	☐	☐	☐	☐	☐	☐
	☐	☐	☐	☐	☐	☐	☐
	☐	☐	☐	☐	☐	☐	☐

03/15 MONDAY

- [ ]
- [ ]
- [ ]
- [ ]
- [ ]
- [ ]
- [ ]
- [ ]
- [ ]
- [ ]
- [ ]
- [ ]
- [ ]
- [ ]
- [ ]

03/16 TUESDAY

- [ ]
- [ ]
- [ ]
- [ ]
- [ ]
- [ ]
- [ ]
- [ ]
- [ ]
- [ ]
- [ ]
- [ ]
- [ ]
- [ ]
- [ ]

03/17 WEDNESDAY

- [ ]
- [ ]
- [ ]
- [ ]
- [ ]
- [ ]
- [ ]
- [ ]
- [ ]
- [ ]
- [ ]
- [ ]
- [ ]
- [ ]
- [ ]
- [ ]

03/18 THURSDAY

- [ ]
- [ ]
- [ ]
- [ ]
- [ ]
- [ ]
- [ ]
- [ ]
- [ ]
- [ ]
- [ ]
- [ ]
- [ ]
- [ ]
- [ ]
- [ ]

WEEKLY PLANNER

03/19 FRIDAY

- [ ]
- [ ]
- [ ]
- [ ]
- [ ]
- [ ]
- [ ]
- [ ]
- [ ]
- [ ]
- [ ]
- [ ]
- [ ]
- [ ]
- [ ]

03/20 SATURDAY

- [ ]
- [ ]
- [ ]
- [ ]
- [ ]
- [ ]

03/21 SUNDAY

- [ ]
- [ ]
- [ ]
- [ ]
- [ ]
- [ ]

APPOINTMENTS

NOTES

TRACKER

	S	M	T	W	T	F	S
	☐	☐	☐	☐	☐	☐	☐
	☐	☐	☐	☐	☐	☐	☐
	☐	☐	☐	☐	☐	☐	☐
	☐	☐	☐	☐	☐	☐	☐
	☐	☐	☐	☐	☐	☐	☐
	☐	☐	☐	☐	☐	☐	☐

03/22 MONDAY

- [ ]
- [ ]
- [ ]
- [ ]
- [ ]
- [ ]
- [ ]
- [ ]
- [ ]
- [ ]
- [ ]
- [ ]
- [ ]
- [ ]
- [ ]

03/23 TUESDAY

- [ ]
- [ ]
- [ ]
- [ ]
- [ ]
- [ ]
- [ ]
- [ ]
- [ ]
- [ ]
- [ ]
- [ ]
- [ ]
- [ ]
- [ ]

03/24 WEDNESDAY

- [ ]
- [ ]
- [ ]
- [ ]
- [ ]
- [ ]
- [ ]
- [ ]
- [ ]
- [ ]
- [ ]
- [ ]
- [ ]
- [ ]
- [ ]
- [ ]

03/25 THURSDAY

- [ ]
- [ ]
- [ ]
- [ ]
- [ ]
- [ ]
- [ ]
- [ ]
- [ ]
- [ ]
- [ ]
- [ ]
- [ ]
- [ ]
- [ ]
- [ ]

WEEKLY PLANNER

03/26 FRIDAY

- [ ]
- [ ]
- [ ]
- [ ]
- [ ]
- [ ]
- [ ]
- [ ]
- [ ]
- [ ]
- [ ]
- [ ]
- [ ]
- [ ]
- [ ]

03/27 SATURDAY

- [ ]
- [ ]
- [ ]
- [ ]
- [ ]
- [ ]

03/28 SUNDAY

- [ ]
- [ ]
- [ ]
- [ ]
- [ ]
- [ ]

APPOINTMENTS

NOTES

TRACKER

	S	M	T	W	T	F	S
	☐	☐	☐	☐	☐	☐	☐
	☐	☐	☐	☐	☐	☐	☐
	☐	☐	☐	☐	☐	☐	☐
	☐	☐	☐	☐	☐	☐	☐
	☐	☐	☐	☐	☐	☐	☐
	☐	☐	☐	☐	☐	☐	☐

03/29 MONDAY

03/30 TUESDAY

03/31 WEDNESDAY

04/01 THURSDAY

WEEKLY PLANNER

04/02 FRIDAY

- [ ]
- [ ]
- [ ]
- [ ]
- [ ]
- [ ]
- [ ]
- [ ]
- [ ]
- [ ]
- [ ]
- [ ]
- [ ]
- [ ]
- [ ]

04/03 SATURDAY

- [ ]
- [ ]
- [ ]
- [ ]
- [ ]
- [ ]

04/04 SUNDAY

- [ ]
- [ ]
- [ ]
- [ ]
- [ ]
- [ ]

APPOINTMENTS

NOTES

TRACKER

	S	M	T	W	T	F	S
	☐	☐	☐	☐	☐	☐	☐
	☐	☐	☐	☐	☐	☐	☐
	☐	☐	☐	☐	☐	☐	☐
	☐	☐	☐	☐	☐	☐	☐
	☐	☐	☐	☐	☐	☐	☐
	☐	☐	☐	☐	☐	☐	☐

I AM A SPARK FROM THE INFINITE

RUMI

April 2021

MARCH

MON	TUE	WED	THU	FRI	SAT	SUN
01	02	03	04	05	06	07
08	09	10	11	12	13	14
15	16	17	18	19	20	21
22	23	24	25	26	27	28
29	30	31				

MONDAY	TUESDAY	WEDNESDAY	THURSDAY	FRIDAY	SATURDAY	SUNDAY
			01	02	03	04
05	06	07	08	09	10	1
12	13	14	15	16	17	18
19	20	21	22	23	24	25
26	27	28	29	30		

MAY

MON	TUE	WED	THU	FRI	SAT	SUN
					01	02
03	04	05	06	07	08	09
10	11	12	13	14	15	16
17	18	19	20	21	22	23
24	25	26	27	28	29	30
31						

BIRTHSTONE: Diamond

ZOIDIAC SIGN: Mar 21 - April 19 Aries
April 20 - May 20 Taurus

BIRTH MONTH FLOWER: Daisy & Sweet Pea

Spiritual Goals

Intentions

Astrological Events

Card of the Mo.

I am grateful for

I am

To Do

- [ ]
- [ ]
- [ ]
- [ ]
- [ ]
- [ ]
- [ ]

To Buy

- [ ]
- [ ]
- [ ]
- [ ]
- [ ]
- [ ]
- [ ]

04/05 MONDAY

04/06 TUESDAY

04/07 WEDNESDAY

04/08 THURSDAY

WEEKLY PLANNER

04/09 FRIDAY

- [ ]
- [ ]
- [ ]
- [ ]
- [ ]
- [ ]
- [ ]
- [ ]
- [ ]
- [ ]
- [ ]
- [ ]
- [ ]
- [ ]
- [ ]

04/10 SATURDAY

- [ ]
- [ ]
- [ ]
- [ ]
- [ ]
- [ ]

04/11 SUNDAY

- [ ]
- [ ]
- [ ]
- [ ]
- [ ]
- [ ]

APPOINTMENTS

NOTES

TRACKER

	S	M	T	W	T	F	S
	☐	☐	☐	☐	☐	☐	☐
	☐	☐	☐	☐	☐	☐	☐
	☐	☐	☐	☐	☐	☐	☐
	☐	☐	☐	☐	☐	☐	☐
	☐	☐	☐	☐	☐	☐	☐
	☐	☐	☐	☐	☐	☐	☐

04/12 MONDAY

- [ ]
- [ ]
- [ ]
- [ ]
- [ ]
- [ ]
- [ ]
- [ ]
- [ ]
- [ ]
- [ ]
- [ ]
- [ ]
- [ ]
- [ ]

04/13 TUESDAY

- [ ]
- [ ]
- [ ]
- [ ]
- [ ]
- [ ]
- [ ]
- [ ]
- [ ]
- [ ]
- [ ]
- [ ]
- [ ]
- [ ]
- [ ]

04/14 WEDNESDAY

- [ ]
- [ ]
- [ ]
- [ ]
- [ ]
- [ ]
- [ ]
- [ ]
- [ ]
- [ ]
- [ ]
- [ ]
- [ ]
- [ ]
- [ ]

04/15 THURSDAY

- [ ]
- [ ]
- [ ]
- [ ]
- [ ]
- [ ]
- [ ]
- [ ]
- [ ]
- [ ]
- [ ]
- [ ]
- [ ]
- [ ]
- [ ]

WEEKLY PLANNER

04/16 FRIDAY

04/17 SATURDAY

04/18 SUNDAY

APPOINTMENTS

NOTES

TRACKER

	S	M	T	W	T	F	S

04/19 MONDAY

- [ ]
- [ ]
- [ ]
- [ ]
- [ ]
- [ ]
- [ ]
- [ ]
- [ ]
- [ ]
- [ ]
- [ ]
- [ ]
- [ ]
- [ ]

04/20 TUESDAY

- [ ]
- [ ]
- [ ]
- [ ]
- [ ]
- [ ]
- [ ]
- [ ]
- [ ]
- [ ]
- [ ]
- [ ]
- [ ]
- [ ]
- [ ]

04/21 WEDNESDAY

- [ ]
- [ ]
- [ ]
- [ ]
- [ ]
- [ ]
- [ ]
- [ ]
- [ ]
- [ ]
- [ ]
- [ ]
- [ ]
- [ ]
- [ ]

04/22 THURSDAY

- [ ]
- [ ]
- [ ]
- [ ]
- [ ]
- [ ]
- [ ]
- [ ]
- [ ]
- [ ]
- [ ]
- [ ]
- [ ]
- [ ]
- [ ]

WEEKLY PLANNER

04/23 FRIDAY

- [ ]
- [ ]
- [ ]
- [ ]
- [ ]
- [ ]
- [ ]
- [ ]
- [ ]
- [ ]
- [ ]
- [ ]
- [ ]
- [ ]
- [ ]

04/24 SATURDAY

- [ ]
- [ ]
- [ ]
- [ ]
- [ ]
- [ ]

04/25 SUNDAY

- [ ]
- [ ]
- [ ]
- [ ]
- [ ]
- [ ]

APPOINTMENTS

NOTES

TRACKER

	S	M	T	W	T	F	S
	☐	☐	☐	☐	☐	☐	☐
	☐	☐	☐	☐	☐	☐	☐
	☐	☐	☐	☐	☐	☐	☐
	☐	☐	☐	☐	☐	☐	☐
	☐	☐	☐	☐	☐	☐	☐
	☐	☐	☐	☐	☐	☐	☐

04/26 MONDAY

04/27 TUESDAY

04/28 WEDNESDAY

04/29 THURSDAY

WEEKLY PLANNER

04/30 FRIDAY

- [ ]
- [ ]
- [ ]
- [ ]
- [ ]
- [ ]
- [ ]
- [ ]
- [ ]
- [ ]
- [ ]
- [ ]
- [ ]
- [ ]
- [ ]

05/01 SATURDAY

- [ ]
- [ ]
- [ ]
- [ ]
- [ ]
- [ ]

05/02 SUNDAY

- [ ]
- [ ]
- [ ]
- [ ]
- [ ]
- [ ]

APPOINTMENTS

NOTES

TRACKER

	S	M	T	W	T	F	S

SHE CONQUERED ALL HER DEMONS AND WORE HER SCARS LIKE WINGS

ATTICUS

APRIL

MON	TUE	WED	THU	FRI	SAT	SUN
			01	02	03	04
05	06	07	08	09	10	11
12	13	14	15	16	17	18
19	20	21	22	23	24	25
26	27	28	29	30		

May 2021

MONDAY	TUESDAY	WEDNESDAY	THURSDAY	FRIDAY	SATURDAY	SUNDAY
					01	02
03	04	05	06	07	08	09
10	11	12	13	14	15	16
17	18	19	20	21	22	23
24 / 31	25	26	27	28	29	30

JUNE

MON	TUE	WED	THU	FRI	SAT	SUN
	01	02	03	04	05	06
07	08	09	10	11	12	13
14	15	16	17	18	19	20
21	22	23	24	25	26	27
28	29	30				

BIRTHSTONE: Emerald, Moonstone, Alexandrite

ZODIAC SIGN: April 20 - May 20 Taurus
May 21 - June 21 Gemini

BIRTH MONTH FLOWER: Lilly Of The Valley
& Hawthorn

Spiritual Goals

Intentions

Astrological Events

Card of the Mo.

I am grateful for

I am

To Do

- [ ]
- [ ]
- [ ]
- [ ]
- [ ]
- [ ]
- [ ]

To Buy

- [ ]
- [ ]
- [ ]
- [ ]
- [ ]
- [ ]
- [ ]

05/03 MONDAY

05/04 TUESDAY

05/05 WEDNESDAY

05/06 THURSDAY

WEEKLY PLANNER

05/07 FRIDAY

05/08 SATURDAY

05/09 SUNDAY

APPOINTMENTS

NOTES

TRACKER

S M T W T F S

05/10 MONDAY

05/11 TUESDAY

05/12 WEDNESDAY

05/13 THURSDAY

WEEKLY PLANNER

05/14 FRIDAY

- [ ]
- [ ]
- [ ]
- [ ]
- [ ]
- [ ]
- [ ]
- [ ]
- [ ]
- [ ]
- [ ]
- [ ]
- [ ]
- [ ]
- [ ]

05/15 SATURDAY

- [ ]
- [ ]
- [ ]
- [ ]
- [ ]
- [ ]

05/16 SUNDAY

- [ ]
- [ ]
- [ ]
- [ ]
- [ ]
- [ ]

APPOINTMENTS

NOTES

TRACKER

	S	M	T	W	T	F	S

05/17 MONDAY

05/18 TUESDAY

05/19 WEDNESDAY

05/20 THURSDAY

WEEKLY PLANNER

05/21 FRIDAY

05/22 SATURDAY

05/23 SUNDAY

APPOINTMENTS

NOTES

TRACKER

	S	M	T	W	T	F	S
	☐	☐	☐	☐	☐	☐	☐
	☐	☐	☐	☐	☐	☐	☐
	☐	☐	☐	☐	☐	☐	☐
	☐	☐	☐	☐	☐	☐	☐
	☐	☐	☐	☐	☐	☐	☐
	☐	☐	☐	☐	☐	☐	☐

05/24 MONDAY

05/25 TUESDAY

05/26 WEDNESDAY

05/27 THURSDAY

WEEKLY PLANNER

05/28 FRIDAY

05/29 SATURDAY

05/30 SUNDAY

APPOINTMENTS

NOTES

TRACKER

	S	M	T	W	T	F	S

AND INTO THE FOREST I GO, TO LOSE MY MIND AND FIND MY SOUL

JOHN MUIR

June 2021

MAY

MON	TUE	WED	THU	FRI	SAT	SUN
					01	02
03	04	05	06	07	08	09
10	11	12	13	14	15	16
17	18	19	20	21	22	23
24	25	26	27	28	29	30
31						

	01	02	03	04	05	0
07	08	09	10	11	12	1
14	15	16	17	18	19	2
21	22	23	24	25	26	2
28	29	30				

JULY

MON	TUE	WED	THU	FRI	SAT	SUN
			01	02	03	04
05	06	07	08	09	10	11
12	13	14	15	16	17	18
19	20	21	22	23	24	25
26	27	28	29	30	31	

BIRTHSTONE: Pearl

ZOIDIAC SIGN: May 21 - June 21 Gemini
June 22 - July 22 Cancer

BIRTH MONTH FLOWER: Rose & Honeysuckle

Spiritual Goals

Intentions

Astrological Events

Card of the Mo.

I am grateful for

I am

To Do

☐
☐
☐
☐
☐
☐
☐

To Buy

☐
☐
☐
☐
☐
☐
☐

05/31 MONDAY

06/01 TUESDAY

06/02 WEDNESDAY

06/03 THURSDAY

WEEKLY PLANNER

06/04 FRIDAY

- [ ]
- [ ]
- [ ]
- [ ]
- [ ]
- [ ]
- [ ]
- [ ]
- [ ]
- [ ]
- [ ]
- [ ]
- [ ]
- [ ]
- [ ]

06/05 SATURDAY

- [ ]
- [ ]
- [ ]
- [ ]
- [ ]
- [ ]

06/06 SUNDAY

- [ ]
- [ ]
- [ ]
- [ ]
- [ ]
- [ ]

APPOINTMENTS

NOTES

TRACKER

	S	M	T	W	T	F	S
	☐	☐	☐	☐	☐	☐	☐
	☐	☐	☐	☐	☐	☐	☐
	☐	☐	☐	☐	☐	☐	☐
	☐	☐	☐	☐	☐	☐	☐
	☐	☐	☐	☐	☐	☐	☐
	☐	☐	☐	☐	☐	☐	☐

06/07 MONDAY

- [ ]
- [ ]
- [ ]
- [ ]
- [ ]
- [ ]
- [ ]
- [ ]
- [ ]
- [ ]
- [ ]
- [ ]
- [ ]
- [ ]
- [ ]

06/08 TUESDAY

- [ ]
- [ ]
- [ ]
- [ ]
- [ ]
- [ ]
- [ ]
- [ ]
- [ ]
- [ ]
- [ ]
- [ ]
- [ ]
- [ ]
- [ ]

06/09 WEDNESDAY

- [ ]
- [ ]
- [ ]
- [ ]
- [ ]
- [ ]
- [ ]
- [ ]
- [ ]
- [ ]
- [ ]
- [ ]
- [ ]
- [ ]
- [ ]
- [ ]

06/10 THURSDAY

- [ ]
- [ ]
- [ ]
- [ ]
- [ ]
- [ ]
- [ ]
- [ ]
- [ ]
- [ ]
- [ ]
- [ ]
- [ ]
- [ ]
- [ ]
- [ ]

WEEKLY PLANNER

06/11 FRIDAY

- [ ]
- [ ]
- [ ]
- [ ]
- [ ]
- [ ]
- [ ]
- [ ]
- [ ]
- [ ]
- [ ]
- [ ]
- [ ]
- [ ]
- [ ]

06/12 SATURDAY

- [ ]
- [ ]
- [ ]
- [ ]
- [ ]
- [ ]

06/13 SUNDAY

- [ ]
- [ ]
- [ ]
- [ ]
- [ ]
- [ ]

APPOINTMENTS

NOTES

TRACKER

	S	M	T	W	T	F	S
	☐	☐	☐	☐	☐	☐	☐
	☐	☐	☐	☐	☐	☐	☐
	☐	☐	☐	☐	☐	☐	☐
	☐	☐	☐	☐	☐	☐	☐
	☐	☐	☐	☐	☐	☐	☐
	☐	☐	☐	☐	☐	☐	☐

06/14 MONDAY

06/15 TUESDAY

06/16 WEDNESDAY

06/17 THURSDAY

WEEKLY PLANNER

06/18 FRIDAY

06/19 SATURDAY

06/20 SUNDAY

APPOINTMENTS

NOTES

TRACKER

	S	M	T	W	T	F	S

06/21 MONDAY

06/22 TUESDAY

06/23 WEDNESDAY

06/24 THURSDAY

WEEKLY PLANNER

06/25 FRIDAY

- [ ]
- [ ]
- [ ]
- [ ]
- [ ]
- [ ]
- [ ]
- [ ]
- [ ]
- [ ]
- [ ]
- [ ]
- [ ]
- [ ]
- [ ]

06/26 SATURDAY

- [ ]
- [ ]
- [ ]
- [ ]
- [ ]
- [ ]

06/27 SUNDAY

- [ ]
- [ ]
- [ ]
- [ ]
- [ ]
- [ ]

APPOINTMENTS

NOTES

TRACKER

	S	M	T	W	T	F	S
	☐	☐	☐	☐	☐	☐	☐
	☐	☐	☐	☐	☐	☐	☐
	☐	☐	☐	☐	☐	☐	☐
	☐	☐	☐	☐	☐	☐	☐
	☐	☐	☐	☐	☐	☐	☐
	☐	☐	☐	☐	☐	☐	☐

06/28 MONDAY

06/29 TUESDAY

06/30 WEDNESDAY

07/01 THURSDAY

WEEKLY PLANNER

07/02 FRIDAY

07/03 SATURDAY

07/04 SUNDAY

APPOINTMENTS

NOTES

TRACKER

	S	M	T	W	T	F	S

THE WORLD IS
FULL OF MAGIC THINGS
PATIENTLY WAITING
FOR OUR SENSES
TO GROW SHARPER

W. B. YEATS

July 2021

JUNE

MON	TUE	WED	THU	FRI	SAT	SU
	01	02	03	04	05	06
07	08	09	10	11	12	13
14	15	16	17	18	19	20
21	22	23	24	25	26	27
28	29	30				

MONDAY	TUESDAY	WEDNESDAY	THURSDAY	FRIDAY	SATURDAY	SUNDAY
			01	02	03	0
05	06	07	08	09	10	1
12	13	14	15	16	17	1
19	20	21	22	23	24	2
26	27	28	29	30	31	

AUGUST

MON	TUE	WED	THU	FRI	SAT	SUN
						01
02	03	04	05	06	07	08
09	10	11	12	13	14	15
16	17	18	19	20	21	22
23	24	25	26	27	28	29
30	31					

BIRTHSTONE: Ruby

ZODIAC SIGN: June 22 - July 22 Cancer
July 23 - Aug 22 Leo

BIRTH MONTH FLOWER: Larkspur & Water Lily

Spiritual Goals

Intentions

Astrological Events

Card of the Mo.

I am grateful for

I am

To Do

☐
☐
☐
☐
☐
☐
☐

To Buy

☐
☐
☐
☐
☐
☐
☐

07/05 MONDAY

- [ ]
- [ ]
- [ ]
- [ ]
- [ ]
- [ ]
- [ ]
- [ ]
- [ ]
- [ ]
- [ ]
- [ ]
- [ ]
- [ ]
- [ ]

07/06 TUESDAY

- [ ]
- [ ]
- [ ]
- [ ]
- [ ]
- [ ]
- [ ]
- [ ]
- [ ]
- [ ]
- [ ]
- [ ]
- [ ]
- [ ]
- [ ]

07/07 WEDNESDAY

- [ ]
- [ ]
- [ ]
- [ ]
- [ ]
- [ ]
- [ ]
- [ ]
- [ ]
- [ ]
- [ ]
- [ ]
- [ ]
- [ ]
- [ ]
- [ ]

07/08 THURSDAY

- [ ]
- [ ]
- [ ]
- [ ]
- [ ]
- [ ]
- [ ]
- [ ]
- [ ]
- [ ]
- [ ]
- [ ]
- [ ]
- [ ]
- [ ]
- [ ]

WEEKLY PLANNER

07/09 FRIDAY

- [ ]
- [ ]
- [ ]
- [ ]
- [ ]
- [ ]
- [ ]
- [ ]
- [ ]
- [ ]
- [ ]
- [ ]
- [ ]
- [ ]
- [ ]

07/10 SATURDAY

- [ ]
- [ ]
- [ ]
- [ ]
- [ ]
- [ ]

07/11 SUNDAY

- [ ]
- [ ]
- [ ]
- [ ]
- [ ]
- [ ]

APPOINTMENTS

NOTES

TRACKER

	S	M	T	W	T	F	S
	☐	☐	☐	☐	☐	☐	☐
	☐	☐	☐	☐	☐	☐	☐
	☐	☐	☐	☐	☐	☐	☐
	☐	☐	☐	☐	☐	☐	☐
	☐	☐	☐	☐	☐	☐	☐
	☐	☐	☐	☐	☐	☐	☐

07/12 MONDAY

07/13 TUESDAY

07/14 WEDNESDAY

07/15 THURSDAY

WEEKLY PLANNER

07/16 FRIDAY

- [ ]
- [ ]
- [ ]
- [ ]
- [ ]
- [ ]
- [ ]
- [ ]
- [ ]
- [ ]
- [ ]
- [ ]
- [ ]
- [ ]
- [ ]

07/17 SATURDAY

- [ ]
- [ ]
- [ ]
- [ ]
- [ ]
- [ ]

07/18 SUNDAY

- [ ]
- [ ]
- [ ]
- [ ]
- [ ]
- [ ]

APPOINTMENTS

NOTES

TRACKER

	S	M	T	W	T	F	S
	☐	☐	☐	☐	☐	☐	☐
	☐	☐	☐	☐	☐	☐	☐
	☐	☐	☐	☐	☐	☐	☐
	☐	☐	☐	☐	☐	☐	☐
	☐	☐	☐	☐	☐	☐	☐
	☐	☐	☐	☐	☐	☐	☐

07/19 MONDAY

07/20 TUESDAY

07/21 WEDNESDAY

07/22 THURSDAY

WEEKLY PLANNER

07/23 FRIDAY

- [ ]
- [ ]
- [ ]
- [ ]
- [ ]
- [ ]
- [ ]
- [ ]
- [ ]
- [ ]
- [ ]
- [ ]
- [ ]
- [ ]
- [ ]

07/24 SATURDAY

- [ ]
- [ ]
- [ ]
- [ ]
- [ ]
- [ ]

07/25 SUNDAY

- [ ]
- [ ]
- [ ]
- [ ]
- [ ]
- [ ]

APPOINTMENTS

NOTES

TRACKER

	S	M	T	W	T	F	S
	☐	☐	☐	☐	☐	☐	☐
	☐	☐	☐	☐	☐	☐	☐
	☐	☐	☐	☐	☐	☐	☐
	☐	☐	☐	☐	☐	☐	☐
	☐	☐	☐	☐	☐	☐	☐
	☐	☐	☐	☐	☐	☐	☐

07/26 MONDAY

- [ ]
- [ ]
- [ ]
- [ ]
- [ ]
- [ ]
- [ ]
- [ ]
- [ ]
- [ ]
- [ ]
- [ ]
- [ ]
- [ ]
- [ ]

07/27 TUESDAY

- [ ]
- [ ]
- [ ]
- [ ]
- [ ]
- [ ]
- [ ]
- [ ]
- [ ]
- [ ]
- [ ]
- [ ]
- [ ]
- [ ]
- [ ]

07/28 WEDNESDAY

- [ ]
- [ ]
- [ ]
- [ ]
- [ ]
- [ ]
- [ ]
- [ ]
- [ ]
- [ ]
- [ ]
- [ ]
- [ ]
- [ ]
- [ ]

07/29 THURSDAY

- [ ]
- [ ]
- [ ]
- [ ]
- [ ]
- [ ]
- [ ]
- [ ]
- [ ]
- [ ]
- [ ]
- [ ]
- [ ]
- [ ]
- [ ]

WEEKLY PLANNER

07/30 FRIDAY

☐ ____
☐ ____
☐ ____
☐ ____
☐ ____
☐ ____
☐ ____
☐ ____
☐ ____
☐ ____
☐ ____
☐ ____
☐ ____
☐ ____
☐ ____

07/31 SATURDAY

☐ ____
☐ ____
☐ ____
☐ ____
☐ ____
☐ ____

08/01 SUNDAY

☐ ____
☐ ____
☐ ____
☐ ____
☐ ____
☐ ____

APPOINTMENTS

NOTES

TRACKER

	S	M	T	W	T	F	S
____	☐	☐	☐	☐	☐	☐	☐
____	☐	☐	☐	☐	☐	☐	☐
____	☐	☐	☐	☐	☐	☐	☐
____	☐	☐	☐	☐	☐	☐	☐
____	☐	☐	☐	☐	☐	☐	☐
____	☐	☐	☐	☐	☐	☐	☐

SOMEWHERE IN THE
GREAT LANDSCAPE OF
TIME THERE IS A GARDEN
GROWING THE MOST
BEAUTIFUL ROSE
THAT HAS EVER BEEN
AND THAT WILL EVER BE
YOU ARE THAT ROSE

ATTICUS

August 2021

JULY

MON	TUE	WED	THU	FRI	SAT	SU
			01	02	03	0
05	06	07	08	09	10	1
12	13	14	15	16	17	1
19	20	21	22	23	24	2
26	27	28	29	30	31	

MONDAY	TUESDAY	WEDNESDAY	THURSDAY	FRIDAY	SATURDAY	SUNDAY
						0
02	03	04	05	06	07	0
09	10	11	12	13	14	1
16	17	18	19	20	21	2
23 / 30	24 / 31	25	26	27	28	2

SEPTEMBER

MON	TUE	WED	THU	FRI	SAT	SUN
		01	02	03	04	05
06	07	08	09	10	11	12
13	14	15	16	17	18	19
20	21	22	23	24	25	26
27	28	29	30			

Magical Monthly Correspondence

BIRTHSTONE: Peridot

ZODIAC SIGN: July 23 - Aug 22 Leo
Aug 23 - Sept 22 Virgo

BIRTH MONTH FLOWER: Gladiolus & Poppy

Spiritual Goals

Intentions

Astrological Events

Card of the Mo.

I am grateful for

I am

To Do

- [ ]
- [ ]
- [ ]
- [ ]
- [ ]
- [ ]
- [ ]

To Buy

- [ ]
- [ ]
- [ ]
- [ ]
- [ ]
- [ ]
- [ ]

08/02 MONDAY

08/03 TUESDAY

08/04 WEDNESDAY

08/05 THURSDAY

WEEKLY PLANNER

08/06 FRIDAY

- [ ]
- [ ]
- [ ]
- [ ]
- [ ]
- [ ]
- [ ]
- [ ]
- [ ]
- [ ]
- [ ]
- [ ]
- [ ]
- [ ]
- [ ]

08/07 SATURDAY

- [ ]
- [ ]
- [ ]
- [ ]
- [ ]
- [ ]

08/08 SUNDAY

- [ ]
- [ ]
- [ ]
- [ ]
- [ ]
- [ ]

APPOINTMENTS

NOTES

TRACKER

	S	M	T	W	T	F	S
	☐	☐	☐	☐	☐	☐	☐
	☐	☐	☐	☐	☐	☐	☐
	☐	☐	☐	☐	☐	☐	☐
	☐	☐	☐	☐	☐	☐	☐
	☐	☐	☐	☐	☐	☐	☐
	☐	☐	☐	☐	☐	☐	☐

08/09 MONDAY

08/10 TUESDAY

08/11 WEDNESDAY

08/12 THURSDAY

WEEKLY PLANNER

08/13 FRIDAY

08/14 SATURDAY

08/15 SUNDAY

APPOINTMENTS

NOTES

TRACKER

	S	M	T	W	T	F	S

08/16 MONDAY

08/17 TUESDAY

08/18 WEDNESDAY

08/19 THURSDAY

WEEKLY PLANNER

08/20 FRIDAY

08/21 SATURDAY

08/22 SUNDAY

APPOINTMENTS

NOTES

TRACKER

	S	M	T	W	T	F	S

08/23 MONDAY

08/24 TUESDAY

08/25 WEDNESDAY

08/26 THURSDAY

WEEKLY PLANNER

08/27 FRIDAY

- [ ]
- [ ]
- [ ]
- [ ]
- [ ]
- [ ]
- [ ]
- [ ]
- [ ]
- [ ]
- [ ]
- [ ]
- [ ]
- [ ]
- [ ]

08/28 SATURDAY

- [ ]
- [ ]
- [ ]
- [ ]
- [ ]
- [ ]

08/29 SUNDAY

- [ ]
- [ ]
- [ ]
- [ ]
- [ ]
- [ ]

APPOINTMENTS

NOTES

TRACKER

	S	M	T	W	T	F	S
	☐	☐	☐	☐	☐	☐	☐
	☐	☐	☐	☐	☐	☐	☐
	☐	☐	☐	☐	☐	☐	☐
	☐	☐	☐	☐	☐	☐	☐
	☐	☐	☐	☐	☐	☐	☐
	☐	☐	☐	☐	☐	☐	☐

LISTEN TO SILENCE IT HAS SO MUCH TO SAY

RUMI

September 2021

AUGUST

MON	TUE	WED	THU	FRI	SAT	SU
						0
02	03	04	05	06	07	0
09	10	11	12	13	14	1
16	17	18	19	20	21	2
23	24	25	26	27	28	2
30	31					

MONDAY	TUESDAY	WEDNESDAY	THURSDAY	FRIDAY	SATURDAY	SUNDAY
		01	02	03	04	0
06	07	08	09	10	11	1
13	14	15	16	17	18	1
20	21	22	23	24	25	2
27	28	29	30			

OCTOBER

MON	TUE	WED	THU	FRI	SAT	SUN
				01	02	03
04	05	06	07	08	09	10
11	12	13	14	15	16	17
18	19	20	21	22	23	24
25	26	27	28	29	30	31

Magical Monthly Correspondence

BIRTHSTONE: Blue Sapphire

ZODIAC SIGN: Aug 23 Sept 22 Virgo
Sept 23 - Oct 23 Libra

BIRTH MONTH FLOWER: Aster & Morning Glory

Spiritual Goals

Intentions

Astrological Events

Card of the Mo.

I am grateful for

I am

To Do

- [ ]
- [ ]
- [ ]
- [ ]
- [ ]
- [ ]
- [ ]

To Buy

- [ ]
- [ ]
- [ ]
- [ ]
- [ ]
- [ ]
- [ ]

08/30 MONDAY

08/31 TUESDAY

09/01 WEDNESDAY

09/02 THURSDAY

WEEKLY PLANNER

09/03 FRIDAY

- [ ]
- [ ]
- [ ]
- [ ]
- [ ]
- [ ]
- [ ]
- [ ]
- [ ]
- [ ]
- [ ]
- [ ]
- [ ]
- [ ]
- [ ]

09/04 SATURDAY

- [ ]
- [ ]
- [ ]
- [ ]
- [ ]
- [ ]

09/05 SUNDAY

- [ ]
- [ ]
- [ ]
- [ ]
- [ ]
- [ ]

APPOINTMENTS

NOTES

TRACKER

	S	M	T	W	T	F	S
	☐	☐	☐	☐	☐	☐	☐
	☐	☐	☐	☐	☐	☐	☐
	☐	☐	☐	☐	☐	☐	☐
	☐	☐	☐	☐	☐	☐	☐
	☐	☐	☐	☐	☐	☐	☐
	☐	☐	☐	☐	☐	☐	☐

09/06 MONDAY

09/07 TUESDAY

09/08 WEDNESDAY

09/09 THURSDAY

WEEKLY PLANNER

09/10 FRIDAY

- [ ]
- [ ]
- [ ]
- [ ]
- [ ]
- [ ]
- [ ]
- [ ]
- [ ]
- [ ]
- [ ]
- [ ]
- [ ]
- [ ]
- [ ]

09/11 SATURDAY

- [ ]
- [ ]
- [ ]
- [ ]
- [ ]
- [ ]

09/12 SUNDAY

- [ ]
- [ ]
- [ ]
- [ ]
- [ ]
- [ ]

APPOINTMENTS

NOTES

TRACKER

	S	M	T	W	T	F	S
	☐	☐	☐	☐	☐	☐	☐
	☐	☐	☐	☐	☐	☐	☐
	☐	☐	☐	☐	☐	☐	☐
	☐	☐	☐	☐	☐	☐	☐
	☐	☐	☐	☐	☐	☐	☐
	☐	☐	☐	☐	☐	☐	☐

09/13 MONDAY

- [ ]
- [ ]
- [ ]
- [ ]
- [ ]
- [ ]
- [ ]
- [ ]
- [ ]
- [ ]
- [ ]
- [ ]
- [ ]
- [ ]
- [ ]

09/14 TUESDAY

- [ ]
- [ ]
- [ ]
- [ ]
- [ ]
- [ ]
- [ ]
- [ ]
- [ ]
- [ ]
- [ ]
- [ ]
- [ ]
- [ ]
- [ ]

09/15 WEDNESDAY

- [ ]
- [ ]
- [ ]
- [ ]
- [ ]
- [ ]
- [ ]
- [ ]
- [ ]
- [ ]
- [ ]
- [ ]
- [ ]
- [ ]
- [ ]
- [ ]

09/16 THURSDAY

- [ ]
- [ ]
- [ ]
- [ ]
- [ ]
- [ ]
- [ ]
- [ ]
- [ ]
- [ ]
- [ ]
- [ ]
- [ ]
- [ ]
- [ ]
- [ ]

WEEKLY PLANNER

09/17 FRIDAY

09/18 SATURDAY

09/19 SUNDAY

APPOINTMENTS

NOTES

TRACKER

S M T W T F S

09/20 MONDAY

09/21 TUESDAY

09/22 WEDNESDAY

09/23 THURSDAY

WEEKLY PLANNER

09/24 FRIDAY

- [ ]
- [ ]
- [ ]
- [ ]
- [ ]
- [ ]
- [ ]
- [ ]
- [ ]
- [ ]
- [ ]
- [ ]
- [ ]
- [ ]
- [ ]

09/25 SATURDAY

- [ ]
- [ ]
- [ ]
- [ ]
- [ ]
- [ ]

09/26 SUNDAY

- [ ]
- [ ]
- [ ]
- [ ]
- [ ]
- [ ]

APPOINTMENTS

NOTES

TRACKER

	S	M	T	W	T	F	S
	☐	☐	☐	☐	☐	☐	☐
	☐	☐	☐	☐	☐	☐	☐
	☐	☐	☐	☐	☐	☐	☐
	☐	☐	☐	☐	☐	☐	☐
	☐	☐	☐	☐	☐	☐	☐
	☐	☐	☐	☐	☐	☐	☐

09/27 MONDAY

- [ ]
- [ ]
- [ ]
- [ ]
- [ ]
- [ ]
- [ ]
- [ ]
- [ ]
- [ ]
- [ ]
- [ ]
- [ ]
- [ ]
- [ ]

09/28 TUESDAY

- [ ]
- [ ]
- [ ]
- [ ]
- [ ]
- [ ]
- [ ]
- [ ]
- [ ]
- [ ]
- [ ]
- [ ]
- [ ]
- [ ]
- [ ]

09/29 WEDNESDAY

- [ ]
- [ ]
- [ ]
- [ ]
- [ ]
- [ ]
- [ ]
- [ ]
- [ ]
- [ ]
- [ ]
- [ ]
- [ ]
- [ ]
- [ ]

09/30 THURSDAY

- [ ]
- [ ]
- [ ]
- [ ]
- [ ]
- [ ]
- [ ]
- [ ]
- [ ]
- [ ]
- [ ]
- [ ]
- [ ]
- [ ]
- [ ]

WEEKLY PLANNER

10/01 FRIDAY

10/02 SATURDAY

10/03 SUNDAY

APPOINTMENTS

NOTES

TRACKER

	S	M	T	W	T	F	S

STOP ACTING SO SMALL, YOU ARE THE UNIVERSE IN ECSTATIC MOTION

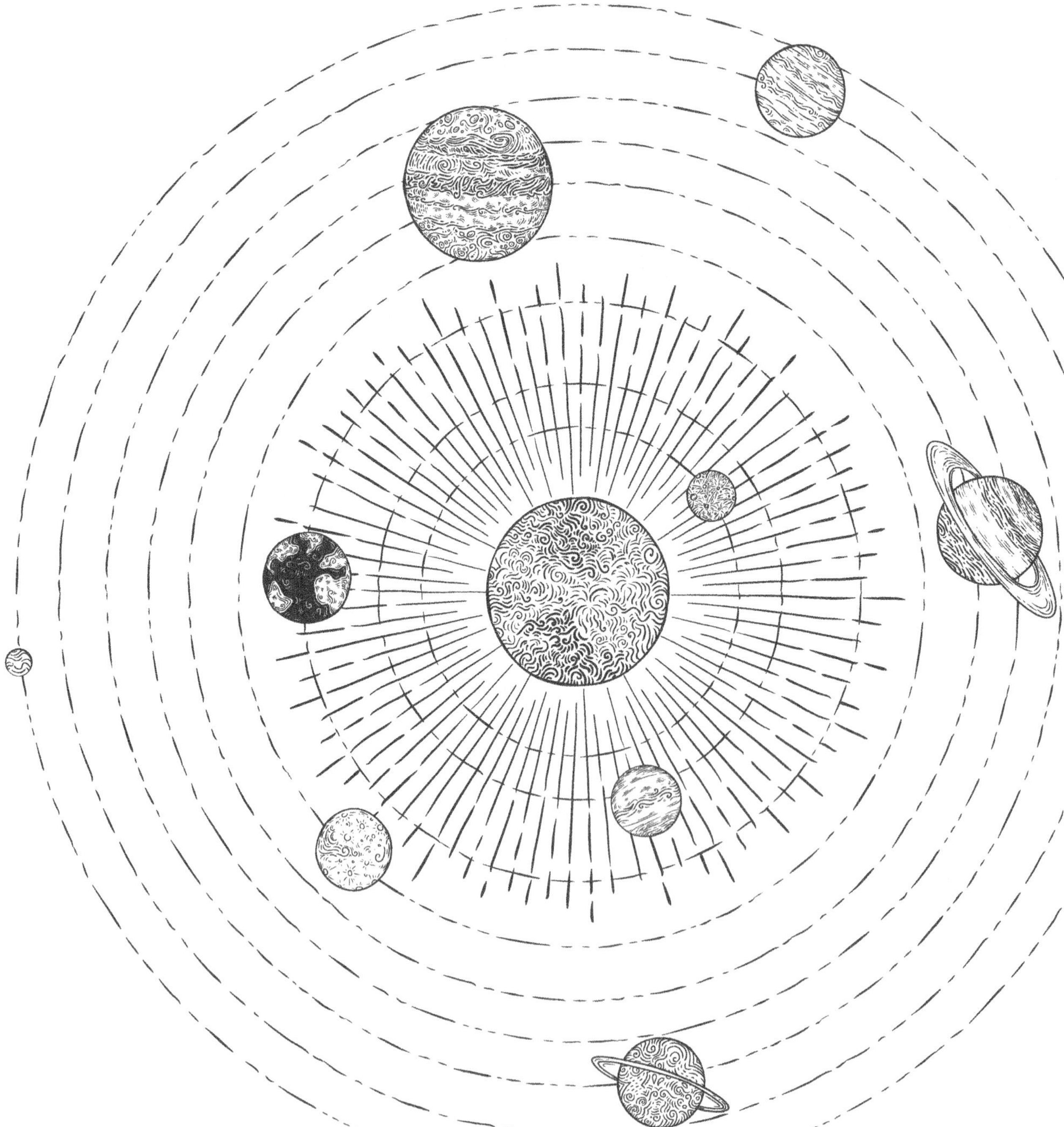

RUMI

October 2021

SEPTEMBER

MON	TUE	WED	THU	FRI	SAT	SU
		01	02	03	04	0
06	07	08	09	10	11	1
13	14	15	16	17	18	1
20	21	22	23	24	25	2
27	28	29	30			

MONDAY	TUESDAY	WEDNESDAY	THURSDAY	FRIDAY	SATURDAY	SUNDAY
				01	02	0
04	05	06	07	08	09	1
11	12	13	14	15	16	1
18	19	20	21	22	23	2
25	26	27	28	29	30	3

NOVEMBER

MON	TUE	WED	THU	FRI	SAT	SUN
01	02	03	04	05	06	07
08	09	10	11	12	13	14
15	16	17	18	19	20	21
22	23	24	25	26	27	28
29	30					

BIRTHSTONE: Opal / Pink Tourmaline

ZOIDIAC SIGN: Sept 23 - Oct 23 Libra
Oct 24 - Nov 21 Scorpio

BIRTH MONTH FLOWER: Marigold & Cosmos

Spiritual Goals

Intentions

Astrological Events

Card of the Mo.

I am grateful for

I am

To Do

☐
☐
☐
☐
☐
☐
☐

To Buy

☐
☐
☐
☐
☐
☐
☐

10/04 MONDAY

10/05 TUESDAY

10/06 WEDNESDAY

10/07 THURSDAY

WEEKLY PLANNER

10/08 FRIDAY

- [ ]
- [ ]
- [ ]
- [ ]
- [ ]
- [ ]
- [ ]
- [ ]
- [ ]
- [ ]
- [ ]
- [ ]
- [ ]
- [ ]
- [ ]

10/09 SATURDAY

- [ ]
- [ ]
- [ ]
- [ ]
- [ ]
- [ ]

10/10 SUNDAY

- [ ]
- [ ]
- [ ]
- [ ]
- [ ]
- [ ]

APPOINTMENTS

NOTES

TRACKER

	S	M	T	W	T	F	S
	☐	☐	☐	☐	☐	☐	☐
	☐	☐	☐	☐	☐	☐	☐
	☐	☐	☐	☐	☐	☐	☐
	☐	☐	☐	☐	☐	☐	☐
	☐	☐	☐	☐	☐	☐	☐
	☐	☐	☐	☐	☐	☐	☐

10/11 MONDAY

- [ ]
- [ ]
- [ ]
- [ ]
- [ ]
- [ ]
- [ ]
- [ ]
- [ ]
- [ ]
- [ ]
- [ ]
- [ ]
- [ ]
- [ ]

10/12 TUESDAY

- [ ]
- [ ]
- [ ]
- [ ]
- [ ]
- [ ]
- [ ]
- [ ]
- [ ]
- [ ]
- [ ]
- [ ]
- [ ]
- [ ]
- [ ]

10/13 WEDNESDAY

- [ ]
- [ ]
- [ ]
- [ ]
- [ ]
- [ ]
- [ ]
- [ ]
- [ ]
- [ ]
- [ ]
- [ ]
- [ ]
- [ ]
- [ ]
- [ ]

10/14 THURSDAY

- [ ]
- [ ]
- [ ]
- [ ]
- [ ]
- [ ]
- [ ]
- [ ]
- [ ]
- [ ]
- [ ]
- [ ]
- [ ]
- [ ]
- [ ]
- [ ]

WEEKLY PLANNER

10/15 FRIDAY

- [ ]
- [ ]
- [ ]
- [ ]
- [ ]
- [ ]
- [ ]
- [ ]
- [ ]
- [ ]
- [ ]
- [ ]
- [ ]
- [ ]
- [ ]

10/16 SATURDAY

- [ ]
- [ ]
- [ ]
- [ ]
- [ ]
- [ ]

10/17 SUNDAY

- [ ]
- [ ]
- [ ]
- [ ]
- [ ]
- [ ]

APPOINTMENTS

NOTES

TRACKER

	S	M	T	W	T	F	S
	☐	☐	☐	☐	☐	☐	☐
	☐	☐	☐	☐	☐	☐	☐
	☐	☐	☐	☐	☐	☐	☐
	☐	☐	☐	☐	☐	☐	☐
	☐	☐	☐	☐	☐	☐	☐
	☐	☐	☐	☐	☐	☐	☐

10/18 MONDAY

- [ ]
- [ ]
- [ ]
- [ ]
- [ ]
- [ ]
- [ ]
- [ ]
- [ ]
- [ ]
- [ ]
- [ ]
- [ ]
- [ ]
- [ ]

10/19 TUESDAY

- [ ]
- [ ]
- [ ]
- [ ]
- [ ]
- [ ]
- [ ]
- [ ]
- [ ]
- [ ]
- [ ]
- [ ]
- [ ]
- [ ]
- [ ]

10/20 WEDNESDAY

- [ ]
- [ ]
- [ ]
- [ ]
- [ ]
- [ ]
- [ ]
- [ ]
- [ ]
- [ ]
- [ ]
- [ ]
- [ ]
- [ ]
- [ ]

10/21 THURSDAY

- [ ]
- [ ]
- [ ]
- [ ]
- [ ]
- [ ]
- [ ]
- [ ]
- [ ]
- [ ]
- [ ]
- [ ]
- [ ]
- [ ]
- [ ]

WEEKLY PLANNER

10/22 FRIDAY

10/23 SATURDAY

10/24 SUNDAY

APPOINTMENTS

NOTES

TRACKER

	S	M	T	W	T	F	S
	☐	☐	☐	☐	☐	☐	☐
	☐	☐	☐	☐	☐	☐	☐
	☐	☐	☐	☐	☐	☐	☐
	☐	☐	☐	☐	☐	☐	☐
	☐	☐	☐	☐	☐	☐	☐
	☐	☐	☐	☐	☐	☐	☐

10/25 MONDAY

10/26 TUESDAY

10/27 WEDNESDAY

10/28 THURSDAY

WEEKLY PLANNER

10/29 FRIDAY

- [ ]
- [ ]
- [ ]
- [ ]
- [ ]
- [ ]
- [ ]
- [ ]
- [ ]
- [ ]
- [ ]
- [ ]
- [ ]
- [ ]
- [ ]

10/30 SATURDAY

- [ ]
- [ ]
- [ ]
- [ ]
- [ ]
- [ ]

10/31 SUNDAY

- [ ]
- [ ]
- [ ]
- [ ]
- [ ]
- [ ]

APPOINTMENTS

NOTES

TRACKER

	S	M	T	W	T	F	S
	☐	☐	☐	☐	☐	☐	☐
	☐	☐	☐	☐	☐	☐	☐
	☐	☐	☐	☐	☐	☐	☐
	☐	☐	☐	☐	☐	☐	☐
	☐	☐	☐	☐	☐	☐	☐
	☐	☐	☐	☐	☐	☐	☐

THE BEST WAY OUT IS ALWAYS THROUGH

ROBERT FROST

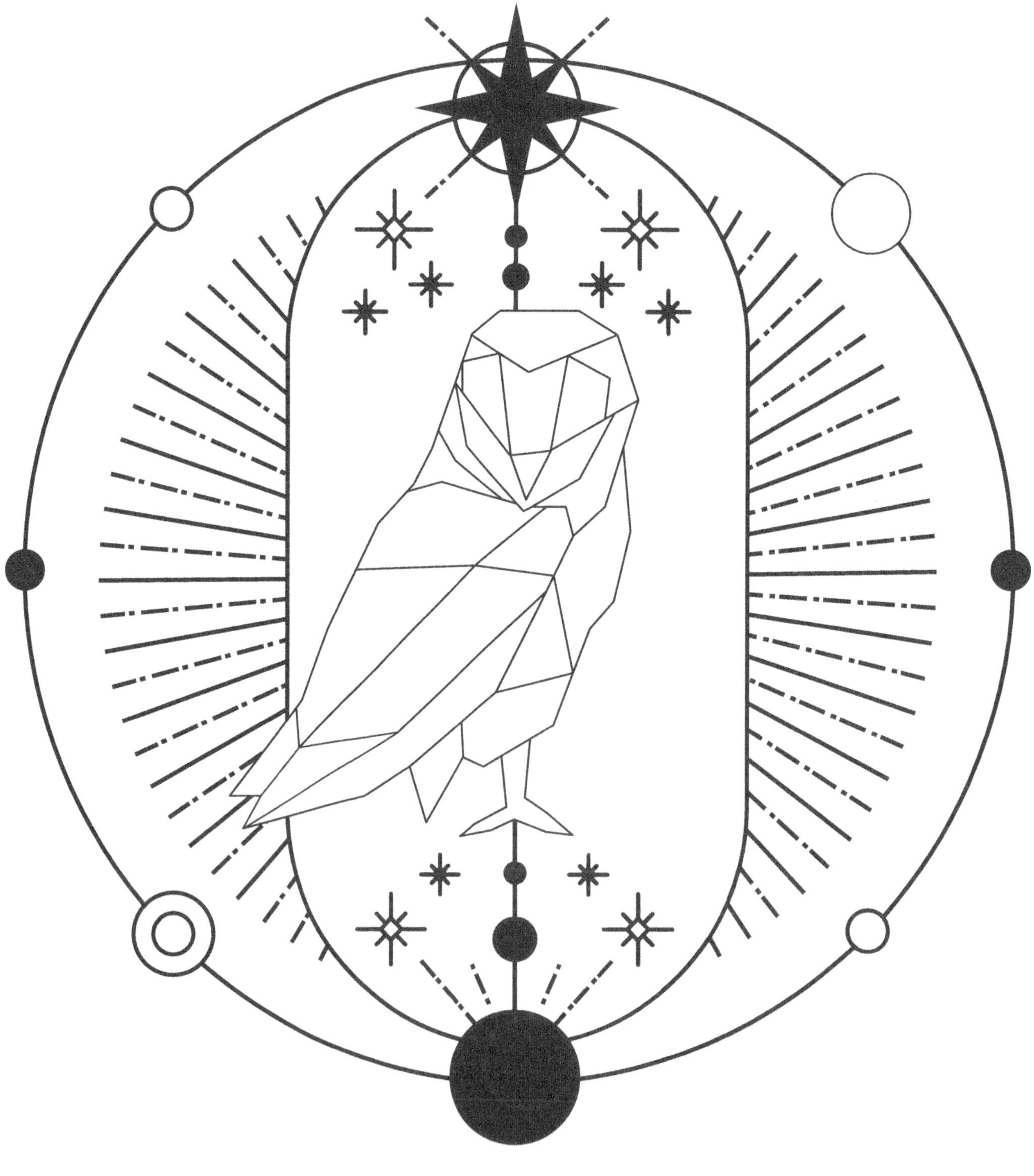

November 2021

OCTOBER

MON	TUE	WED	THU	FRI	SAT	SU
				01	02	03
04	05	06	07	08	09	10
11	12	13	14	15	16	17
18	19	20	21	22	23	24
25	26	27	28	29	30	31

MONDAY	TUESDAY	WEDNESDAY	THURSDAY	FRIDAY	SATURDAY	SUNDAY
01	02	03	04	05	06	0
08	09	10	11	12	13	1
15	16	17	18	19	20	2
22	23	24	25	26	27	2
29	30					

DECEMBER

ION	TUE	WED	THU	FRI	SAT	SUN
		01	02	03	04	05
06	07	08	09	10	11	12
13	14	15	16	17	18	19
20	21	22	23	24	25	26
27	28	29	30	31		

BIRTHSTONE: Citrine, Topaz

ZOIDIAC SIGN: Oct 24 - Nov 21 Scorpio
Nov 22 - Dec 21 Sagittarius

BIRTH MONTH FLOWER: Chrysanthemum

Spiritual Goals

Intentions

Astrological Events

Card of the Mo.

am grateful for

am

To Do

To Buy

11/01 MONDAY

11/02 TUESDAY

11/03 WEDNESDAY

11/04 THURSDAY

WEEKLY PLANNER

11/05 FRIDAY

- [ ]
- [ ]
- [ ]
- [ ]
- [ ]
- [ ]
- [ ]
- [ ]
- [ ]
- [ ]
- [ ]
- [ ]
- [ ]
- [ ]
- [ ]

11/06 SATURDAY

- [ ]
- [ ]
- [ ]
- [ ]
- [ ]
- [ ]

11/07 SUNDAY

- [ ]
- [ ]
- [ ]
- [ ]
- [ ]
- [ ]

APPOINTMENTS

NOTES

TRACKER

	S	M	T	W	T	F	S
	☐	☐	☐	☐	☐	☐	☐
	☐	☐	☐	☐	☐	☐	☐
	☐	☐	☐	☐	☐	☐	☐
	☐	☐	☐	☐	☐	☐	☐
	☐	☐	☐	☐	☐	☐	☐
	☐	☐	☐	☐	☐	☐	☐

11/08 MONDAY

11/09 TUESDAY

11/10 WEDNESDAY

11/11 THURSDAY

WEEKLY PLANNER

11/12 FRIDAY

11/13 SATURDAY

11/14 SUNDAY

APPOINTMENTS

NOTES

TRACKER

	S	M	T	W	T	F	S

11/15 MONDAY

11/16 TUESDAY

11/17 WEDNESDAY

11/18 THURSDAY

WEEKLY PLANNER

11/19 FRIDAY

- [ ]
- [ ]
- [ ]
- [ ]
- [ ]
- [ ]
- [ ]
- [ ]
- [ ]
- [ ]
- [ ]
- [ ]
- [ ]
- [ ]
- [ ]

11/20 SATURDAY

- [ ]
- [ ]
- [ ]
- [ ]
- [ ]
- [ ]

11/21 SUNDAY

- [ ]
- [ ]
- [ ]
- [ ]
- [ ]
- [ ]

APPOINTMENTS

NOTES

TRACKER

	S	M	T	W	T	F	S
	☐	☐	☐	☐	☐	☐	☐
	☐	☐	☐	☐	☐	☐	☐
	☐	☐	☐	☐	☐	☐	☐
	☐	☐	☐	☐	☐	☐	☐
	☐	☐	☐	☐	☐	☐	☐
	☐	☐	☐	☐	☐	☐	☐

11/22 MONDAY

- [ ]
- [ ]
- [ ]
- [ ]
- [ ]
- [ ]
- [ ]
- [ ]
- [ ]
- [ ]
- [ ]
- [ ]
- [ ]
- [ ]
- [ ]

11/23 TUESDAY

- [ ]
- [ ]
- [ ]
- [ ]
- [ ]
- [ ]
- [ ]
- [ ]
- [ ]
- [ ]
- [ ]
- [ ]
- [ ]
- [ ]
- [ ]

11/24 WEDNESDAY

- [ ]
- [ ]
- [ ]
- [ ]
- [ ]
- [ ]
- [ ]
- [ ]
- [ ]
- [ ]
- [ ]
- [ ]
- [ ]
- [ ]
- [ ]
- [ ]

11/25 THURSDAY

- [ ]
- [ ]
- [ ]
- [ ]
- [ ]
- [ ]
- [ ]
- [ ]
- [ ]
- [ ]
- [ ]
- [ ]
- [ ]
- [ ]
- [ ]
- [ ]

WEEKLY PLANNER

11/26 FRIDAY

11/27 SATURDAY

11/28 SUNDAY

APPOINTMENTS

NOTES

TRACKER

	S	M	T	W	T	F	S
	☐	☐	☐	☐	☐	☐	☐
	☐	☐	☐	☐	☐	☐	☐
	☐	☐	☐	☐	☐	☐	☐
	☐	☐	☐	☐	☐	☐	☐
	☐	☐	☐	☐	☐	☐	☐
	☐	☐	☐	☐	☐	☐	☐

11/29 MONDAY

- [ ]
- [ ]
- [ ]
- [ ]
- [ ]
- [ ]
- [ ]
- [ ]
- [ ]
- [ ]
- [ ]
- [ ]
- [ ]
- [ ]
- [ ]

11/30 TUESDAY

- [ ]
- [ ]
- [ ]
- [ ]
- [ ]
- [ ]
- [ ]
- [ ]
- [ ]
- [ ]
- [ ]
- [ ]
- [ ]
- [ ]
- [ ]

12/01 WEDNESDAY

- [ ]
- [ ]
- [ ]
- [ ]
- [ ]
- [ ]
- [ ]
- [ ]
- [ ]
- [ ]
- [ ]
- [ ]
- [ ]
- [ ]
- [ ]
- [ ]

12/02 THURSDAY

- [ ]
- [ ]
- [ ]
- [ ]
- [ ]
- [ ]
- [ ]
- [ ]
- [ ]
- [ ]
- [ ]
- [ ]
- [ ]
- [ ]
- [ ]
- [ ]

WEEKLY PLANNER

12/03 FRIDAY

12/04 SATURDAY

12/05 SUNDAY

APPOINTMENTS

NOTES

TRACKER

	S	M	T	W	T	F	S

IT IS BETTER TO LIGHT ONE SMALL CANDLE THAN TO CURSE THE DARKNESS

CONFUCIUS

December 2021

NOVEMBER

MON	TUE	WED	THU	FRI	SAT	SU
01	02	03	04	05	06	0
08	09	10	11	12	13	1
15	16	17	18	19	20	2
22	23	24	25	26	27	2
29	30					

MONDAY	TUESDAY	WEDNESDAY	THURSDAY	FRIDAY	SATURDAY	SUNDAY
		01	02	03	04	0
06	07	08	09	10	11	1
13	14	15	16	17	18	1
20	21	22	23	24	25	2
27	28	29	30	31		

JANUARY 2022

MON	TUE	WED	THU	FRI	SAT	SUN
					01	02
03	04	05	06	07	08	09
10	11	12	13	14	15	16
17	18	19	20	21	22	23
24	25	26	27	28	29	30
31						

BIRTHSTONE: Blue Zircon, Tanzanite, Turquoise

ZOIDIAC SIGN: Nov 22 - Dec 21 Sagittarius
Dec 22 - Jan 19 Capricorn

BIRTH MONTH FLOWER: Narcissus & Holly

Spiritual Goals

Intentions

Astrological Events

Card of the Mo.

I am grateful for

I am

To Do

☐
☐
☐
☐
☐
☐
☐

To Buy

☐
☐
☐
☐
☐
☐
☐

12/06 MONDAY

- [ ]
- [ ]
- [ ]
- [ ]
- [ ]
- [ ]
- [ ]
- [ ]
- [ ]
- [ ]
- [ ]
- [ ]
- [ ]
- [ ]
- [ ]

12/07 TUESDAY

- [ ]
- [ ]
- [ ]
- [ ]
- [ ]
- [ ]
- [ ]
- [ ]
- [ ]
- [ ]
- [ ]
- [ ]
- [ ]
- [ ]
- [ ]

12/08 WEDNESDAY

- [ ]
- [ ]
- [ ]
- [ ]
- [ ]
- [ ]
- [ ]
- [ ]
- [ ]
- [ ]
- [ ]
- [ ]
- [ ]
- [ ]
- [ ]

12/09 THURSDAY

- [ ]
- [ ]
- [ ]
- [ ]
- [ ]
- [ ]
- [ ]
- [ ]
- [ ]
- [ ]
- [ ]
- [ ]
- [ ]
- [ ]
- [ ]

WEEKLY PLANNER

12/10 FRIDAY

- [ ]
- [ ]
- [ ]
- [ ]
- [ ]
- [ ]
- [ ]
- [ ]
- [ ]
- [ ]
- [ ]
- [ ]
- [ ]
- [ ]
- [ ]

12/11 SATURDAY

- [ ]
- [ ]
- [ ]
- [ ]
- [ ]
- [ ]

12/12 SUNDAY

- [ ]
- [ ]
- [ ]
- [ ]
- [ ]
- [ ]

APPOINTMENTS

NOTES

TRACKER

	S	M	T	W	T	F	S
	☐	☐	☐	☐	☐	☐	☐
	☐	☐	☐	☐	☐	☐	☐
	☐	☐	☐	☐	☐	☐	☐
	☐	☐	☐	☐	☐	☐	☐
	☐	☐	☐	☐	☐	☐	☐
	☐	☐	☐	☐	☐	☐	☐

12/13 MONDAY

12/14 TUESDAY

12/15 WEDNESDAY

12/16 THURSDAY

WEEKLY PLANNER

12/17 FRIDAY

- [ ]
- [ ]
- [ ]
- [ ]
- [ ]
- [ ]
- [ ]
- [ ]
- [ ]
- [ ]
- [ ]
- [ ]
- [ ]
- [ ]
- [ ]

12/18 SATURDAY

- [ ]
- [ ]
- [ ]
- [ ]
- [ ]
- [ ]

12/19 SUNDAY

- [ ]
- [ ]
- [ ]
- [ ]
- [ ]
- [ ]

APPOINTMENTS

NOTES

TRACKER

	S	M	T	W	T	F	S
	☐	☐	☐	☐	☐	☐	☐
	☐	☐	☐	☐	☐	☐	☐
	☐	☐	☐	☐	☐	☐	☐
	☐	☐	☐	☐	☐	☐	☐
	☐	☐	☐	☐	☐	☐	☐
	☐	☐	☐	☐	☐	☐	☐

12/20 MONDAY

12/21 TUESDAY

12/22 WEDNESDAY

12/23 THURSDAY

WEEKLY PLANNER

12/24 FRIDAY

12/25 SATURDAY

12/26 SUNDAY

APPOINTMENTS

NOTES

TRACKER

	S	M	T	W	T	F	S

12/27 MONDAY

- [ ]
- [ ]
- [ ]
- [ ]
- [ ]
- [ ]
- [ ]
- [ ]
- [ ]
- [ ]
- [ ]
- [ ]
- [ ]
- [ ]
- [ ]

12/28 TUESDAY

- [ ]
- [ ]
- [ ]
- [ ]
- [ ]
- [ ]
- [ ]
- [ ]
- [ ]
- [ ]
- [ ]
- [ ]
- [ ]
- [ ]
- [ ]

12/29 WEDNESDAY

- [ ]
- [ ]
- [ ]
- [ ]
- [ ]
- [ ]
- [ ]
- [ ]
- [ ]
- [ ]
- [ ]
- [ ]
- [ ]
- [ ]
- [ ]
- [ ]

12/30 THURSDAY

- [ ]
- [ ]
- [ ]
- [ ]
- [ ]
- [ ]
- [ ]
- [ ]
- [ ]
- [ ]
- [ ]
- [ ]
- [ ]
- [ ]
- [ ]
- [ ]

WEEKLY PLANNER

12/30 FRIDAY

- [ ]
- [ ]
- [ ]
- [ ]
- [ ]
- [ ]
- [ ]
- [ ]
- [ ]
- [ ]
- [ ]
- [ ]
- [ ]
- [ ]
- [ ]

12/31 SATURDAY

- [ ]
- [ ]
- [ ]
- [ ]
- [ ]
- [ ]

01/01 SUNDAY

- [ ]
- [ ]
- [ ]
- [ ]
- [ ]
- [ ]

APPOINTMENTS

NOTES

TRACKER

	S	M	T	W	T	F	S
	☐	☐	☐	☐	☐	☐	☐
	☐	☐	☐	☐	☐	☐	☐
	☐	☐	☐	☐	☐	☐	☐
	☐	☐	☐	☐	☐	☐	☐
	☐	☐	☐	☐	☐	☐	☐
	☐	☐	☐	☐	☐	☐	☐

Made in the USA
Monee, IL
31 July 2021

74635211R00090